Ludwig van Beethoven

COMPLETE STRING QUARTETS

AND GROSSE FUGE

— • —

FROM THE BREITKOPF & HÄRTEL
COMPLETE WORKS EDITION

DOVER PUBLICATIONS, INC.
NEW YORK

This Dover edition, first published in 1970, is an unabridged republication of *Serie 6* (Volumes 1 and 2): *Quartette für 2 Violinen, Bratsche und Violoncell* of *Ludwig van Beethoven's Werke. Vollständige kritisch durchgesehene überall berechtigte Ausgabe. Mit Genehmigung aller Originalverleger,* originally published by Breitkopf & Härtel, Leipzig, n.d.

The publisher is grateful to the Sibley Music Library of the Eastman School of Music, Rochester, N.Y., for making its material available for reproduction.

Library of Congress Catalog Card Number: 75–104809

International Standard Book Number

ISBN-13: 978-0-486-22361-2
ISBN-10: 0-486-22361-2

Manufactured in the United States by LSC Communications
22361232   2019
www.doverpublications.com

Contents

Ludwig van Beethoven's Werke.

Vollständige kritisch durchgesehene überall berechtigte Ausgabe.

Mit Genehmigung aller Originalverleger.

Serie 6.

QUARTETTE
für 2 Violinen, Bratsche und Violoncell.

PARTITUR.

Erster Band.

Leipzig, Verlag von Breitkopf & Härtel.

SECHS QUARTETTE
für 2 Violinen, Bratsche und Violoncell
von
L. van BEETHOVEN.

Dem Fürsten von Lobkowitz gewidmet.
Op. 18. No 1.

Beethovens Werke.

Serie 6. No 37.

Quartett No 1.

Allegro con brio.

Stich und Druck von Breitkopf & Härtel in Leipzig.

Adagio affettuoso ed appassionato.

SCHERZO.
Allegro molto.

Trio.

Beethovens Werke.

SECHS QUARTETTE
für 2 Violinen, Bratsche und Violoncell
von
L. van BEETHOVEN.

Dem Fürsten von Lobkowitz gewidmet.
Op. 18. N.º 2.

Quartett N.º 2.

Stich und Druck von Breitkopf & Härtel in Leipzig.

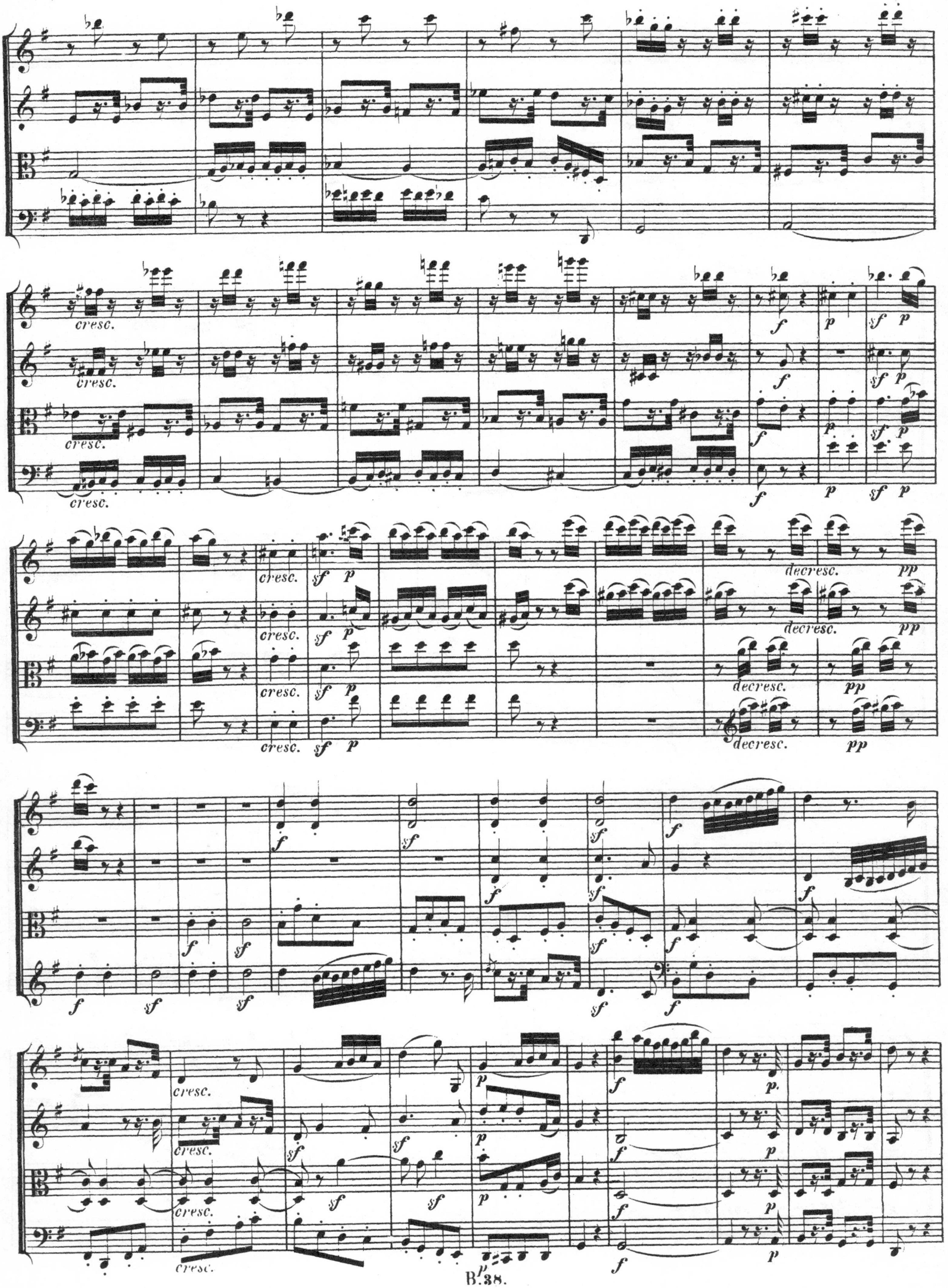
cresc.
decresc.
f
p
sf
pp

B.38.

Tempo I.

Scherzo Allegro.

Trio.

Scherzo D.C.

Allegro molto quasi Presto.

SECHS QUARTETTE
für 2 Violinen, Bratsche und Violoncell
von
L. van BEETHOVEN.
Dem Fürsten von Lobkowitz gewidmet.
Op. 18. No 3.

Beethovens Werke.

Serie 6. No 39.

Quartett No 3.

Stich und Druck von Breitkopf & Härtel in Leipzig.

B.39.

Andante con moto.

B.39.

Allegro.

Minore.

Presto.

SECHS QUARTETTE

von

L. VAN BEETHOVEN.

Beethovens Werke.

Serie 6. No 40.

Dem Fürsten von Lobkowitz gewidmet.

Op.18. No 4.

Quartett No 4.

Stich und Druck von Breitkopf & Härtel in Leipzig.

SCHERZO.
Andante scherzoso quasi Allegretto.

MENUETTO.
Allegretto.

Trio.

La seconda volta si prende
il Tempo più Allegro.

Men. D.C.

Allegro.

Prestissimo.

SECHS QUARTETTE
von
L. van BEETHOVEN.

Beethovens Werke.

Dem Fürsten von Lobkowitz gewidmet.

Op. 18. No 5.

Quartett No. 5.

MENUETTO.

Trio.

Menuetto D. C.

Andante cantabile.

Var. 1.

Var. 2.

Var. 3.

Poco Adagio.

Allegro.

SECHS QUARTETTE
von
L. van BEETHOVEN.

Beethovens Werke.

Dem Fürsten von Lobkowitz gewidmet.

Quartett No 6.

Op.18. No 6.

Allegro con brio.

Stich und Druck von Breitkopf & Härtel in Leipzig.

Adagio ma non troppo.

queste note ben marcate.

queste note ben marcato.

cresc.

SCHERZO.
Allegro.

Trio.

Scherzo D.C.

LA MALINCONIA.

Questo pezzo si deve trattare colla più gran delicatezza.

Adagio.

Allegretto quasi Allegro.

attacca subito il Allegretto.

Tempo I.

Allegretto.

Adagio. Allegretto.

poco Adagio.

Prestissimo.

DREI QUARTETTE
für 2 Violinen, Bratsche und Violoncell
von
L. VAN BEETHOVEN.

Beethovens Werke.

Serie 6. № 43.

Dem Grafen Rasoumoffsky gewidmet.

Op.59. № 1.

Quartett № 7.

Stich und Druck von Breitkopf & Härtel in Leipzig.

B.43.

Allegretto vivace e sempre scherzando.

B.43.

Adagio molto e mesto.

Thème russe.
Allegro.

B. 43.

DREI QUARTETTE
für 2 Violinen, Bratsche und Violoncell
von
L. VAN BEETHOVEN.

Beethovens Werke.

Dem Grafen Rasoumoffsky gewidmet.
Op. 59. No. 2.

Quartett No. 8.

Stich und Druck von Breitkopf & Härtel in Leipzig.

pp
cresc.
il
più
f
ff
sempre ff
sempre p
poco ritard
poco ritard.
a tempo.
cresc.

Molto Adagio. Si tratta questo pezzo con molto di sentimento.

Da capo il minore ma senza replica ed allora ancora una volta il trio, e dopo di nuovo da capo il minore senza replica

Finale. Presto.

B.11.

DREI QUARTETTE
für 2 Violinen, Bratsche und Violoncell
von
L. van BEETHOVEN.

Beethovens Werke.

Serie 6. N⁰ 45.

Dem Grafen Rasoumoffsky gewidmet.

Quartett N⁰ 9.

Op. 59. N⁰ 3.

Introduzione.
Andante con moto.

Violino I.

Violino II.

Viola.

Violoncello.

Allegro vivace.

Stich und Druck von Breitkopf & Härtel in Leipzig.

B. 45.

Andante con moto quasi Allegretto.

B. 45

B.45.

Menuetto. Grazioso.

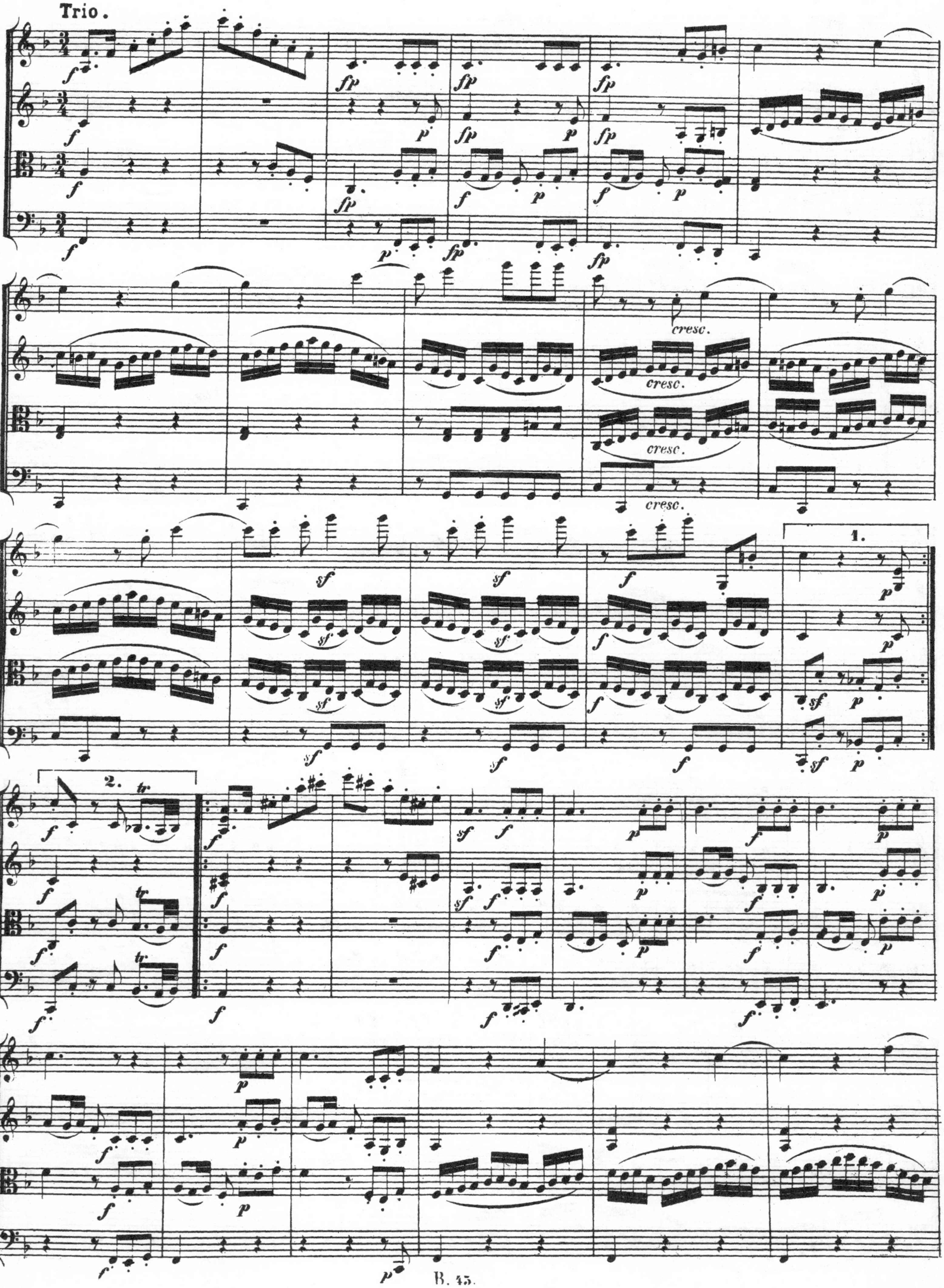
Trio.

Menuetto da Capo.

Coda.

B. 45.

attacca subito.

Allegro molto.

B.45.

B. 45.

Ludwig van Beethovens Werke.

Vollständige kritisch durchgesehene überall berechtigte Ausgabe.
Mit Genehmigung aller Originalverleger.

Serie 6.

QUARTETTE
für 2 Violinen, Bratsche und Violoncell.

PARTITUR.

Zweiter Band.

Leipzig, Verlag von Breitkopf & Härtel.

Die Resultate der kritischen Revision dieser Ausgabe sind Eigenthum der Verleger.

QUARTETT
für 2 Violinen, Bratsche und Violoncell
von
L. van BEETHOVEN.

Dem Fürsten von Lobkowitz gewidmet.

Op. 74.

Beethovens Werke.

Serie 6. Nº 46.

Quartett Nº 10.

Componirt im Jahre 1809.

Original-Verleger: Breitkopf & Härtel in Leipzig.

B. 46.

Stich und Druck von Breitkopf & Härtel in Leipzig.

B.46.

B.46.

Adagio ma non troppo.

B.46.

B.46.

B.46.

Più presto quasi prestissimo.

Si ha s'immaginar la battuta di $\frac{6}{8}$.

Tempo I.

Più presto quasi prestissimo.

B.46.

Tempo I.

B. 46.

attacca il Tema dei Variazioni.

Allegretto con Variazioni.

un poco più vivace.

B.46.

QUARTETT
für 2 Violinen, Bratsche und Violoncell
von
L. van BEETHOVEN.

Beethovens Werke.

Serie 6. No 47.

Nik. Zmeskall von Domanovetz gewidmet.

Op. 95.

Quartett No 11.

Allegro con brio.

Componirt im October 1810.

Original-Verleger: C. Haslinger qm Tobias in Wien. B. 47. Stich und Druck von Breitkopf & Härtel in Leipzig.

Allegretto ma non troppo.

B. 47.

Allegro assai vivace ma serioso.

B.47.

Più Allegro.

Larghetto espressivo.

Allegretto agitato.

B. 47.

B. 47.

QUARTETT
für 2 Violinen, Bratsche und Violoncell
von
L. van BEETHOVEN.

Beethovens Werke.

Serie 6. No 48.

Dem Fürsten Nicolaus von Galitzin gewidmet.

Quartett No 12.

.Op. 127.

Componirt im Jahre 1824.

Original-Verleger: B. Schott Söhne in Mainz.

B. 48

Stich und Druck von Breitkopf & Härtel in Leipzig.

Maestoso.

Allo.

Adagio, ma non troppo e molto cantabile.

Andante con moto.

B.48.

B.48.

Tempo I.

Tempo I.

Finale.

sul G.

Allegro con moto.

QUARTETT

für 2 Violinen, Bratsche und Violoncell

Beethovens Werke.

L. van BEETHOVEN.

Dem Fürsten Nicolaus von Galitzin gewidmet.

Op. 130.

Quartett No 13.

Original-Verleger: C. Haslinger qm Tobias in Wien.   B. 49.   Stich und Druck von Breitkopf & Härtel in Leipzig.

Tempo I.

Allegro.

Allegro.

B.49.

B. 49.

B. 49.

Andante con moto ma non troppo.
Poco scherzoso.

B.49.

B.49.

B.49.

Alla danza tedesca.

Allegro assai.

Cavatina.
Adagio molto espressivo.

Finale.
Allegro.

B.49.

B.49.

B. 49.

B.49.

B.49.

B. 49.

QUARTETT
für 2 Violinen, Bratsche und Violoncell

Beethovens Werke.

von
L. van BEETHOVEN.

Dem Baron von Stutterheim gewidmet.

Op.131.

Quartett No. 14.

No 1. Adagio ma non troppo e molto espressivo.

Violino I.

Violino II.

Viola.

Violoncello.

Original-Verleger: B. Schott Söhne in Mainz.

Stich und Druck von Breitkopf & Härtel in Leipzig.

B.50.

Nº 2. Allegro molto vivace.

Nº 3. Allegro moderato.

Nᵒ 4. Andante ma non troppo e molto cantabile.

Più mosso.

B.50.

Andante moderato e lusinghiero.

Allegretto.

B.50.

Adagio ma non troppo e semplice.

B.50.

Nº 5. Presto.

B.50.

№ 6. Adagio quasi un poco andante.

№ 7. Allegro.

B.50.

B 50.

Poco adagio.

Tempo I.

B. 50.

QUARTETT
für 2 Violinen, Bratsche und Violoncell
von
L. van BEETHOVEN.

Beethovens Werke.

Serie 6. No. 51.

Dem Fürsten Nicolaus von Galitzin gewidmet.

Op. 132.

Quartett No 15.

Componirt im Jahre 1825.

Original-Verleger: A.M. Schlesinger in Berlin.

B. 51.

Stich und Druck von Breitkopf & Härtel in Leipzig.

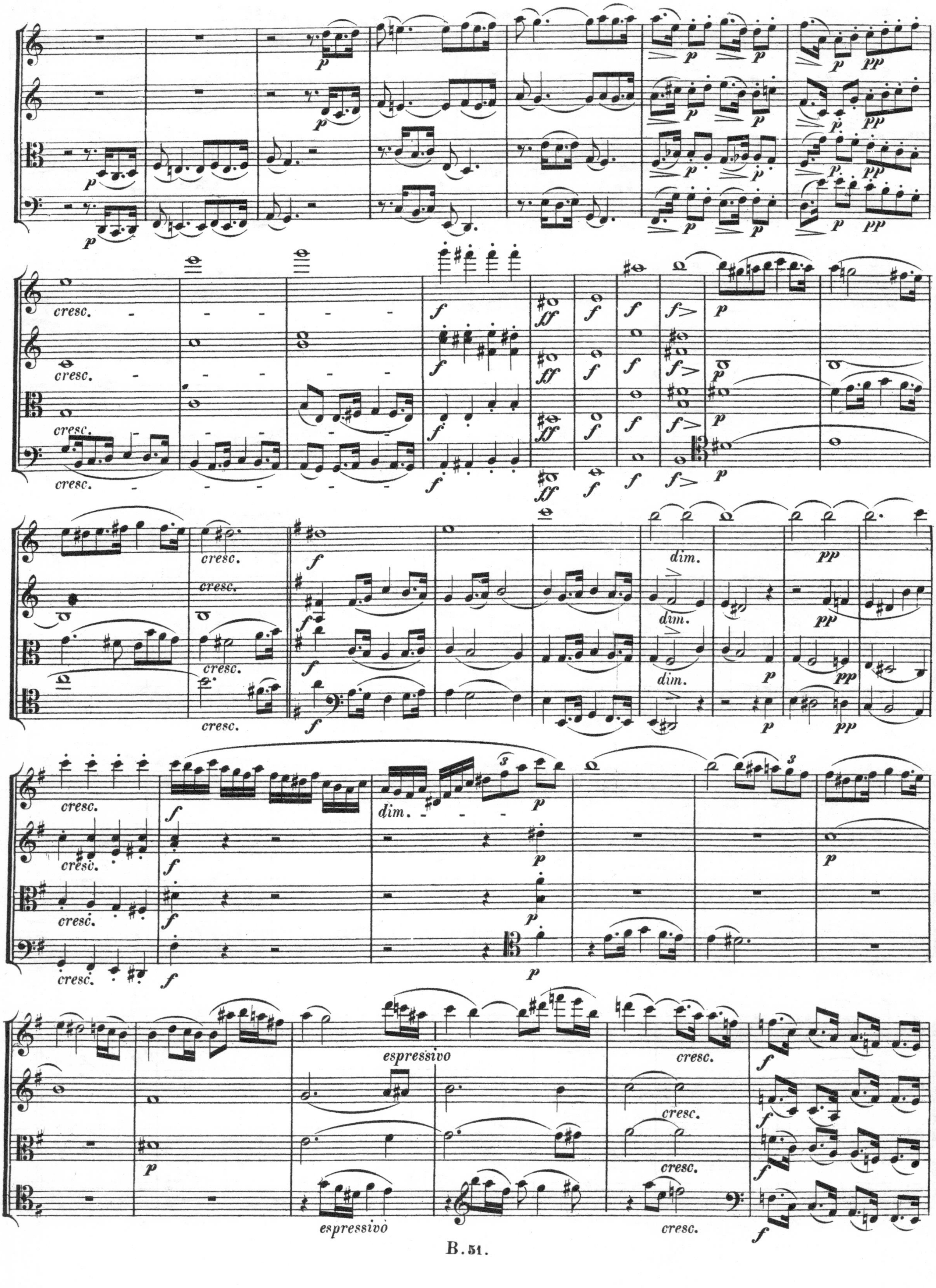
cresc.
dim.
espressivo

B.51.

Allegro ma non tanto.

D.C. al Fine.

Heiliger Dankgesang eines Genesenen an die Gottheit, in der lydischen Tonart.
(Canzona di ringraziamento offerta alla divinità da un guarito, in modo lidico.)

Molto adagio.

Neue Kraft fühlend.
(Sentendo nuova forza.)
Andante.

NB. Die deutschen Ueberschriften sind von Beethovens Hand, die italienischen von fremder Hand im Originalmanuscript geschrieben.

B. 51.

B.51.

Alla Marcia, assai vivace.

B. 51.

Allegro appassionato.

B. 51.

B.51.

QUARTETT
für 2 Violinen, Bratsche und Violoncell
von
L. van BEETHOVEN.

Johann Wolfmeier gewidmet.
Op.135.
(Nachgelassenes Werk.)

Beethovens Werke.

Serie 6. No. 52.

Quartett No. 16.

Componirt im October 1826.

Original-Verleger: A.M.Schlesinger in Berlin.   B.52.   Stich und Druck von Breitkopf & Härtel in Leipzig.

Vivace.

B.52.

Lento assai, cantante e tranquillo.

Più lento.

Tempo I.

DER SCHWER GEFASSTE ENTSCHLUSS.

Grave.   **Allegro.**

Muss es sein?   Es muss sein!   Es muss sein!

Grave ma non troppo tratto.

Grave ma non troppo tratto.

GROSSE FUGE

(Grande Fugue, tantôt libre, tantôt recherchée)

Beethovens Werke.

Serie 6. N° 53.

für 2 Violinen, Bratsche und Violoncell
von
L. van BEETHOVEN.

Dem Cardinal Erzherzog Rudolph gewidmet.

Overtura.
Allegro.

Op. 133.

Violino I.

Violino II.

Viola.

Violoncello.

Meno mosso e moderato.

Allegro.

Fuga.

Original-Verleger: C. Häslinger qm Tobias in Wien.

B. 53.

Stich und Druck von Breitkopf & Härtel in Leipzig.

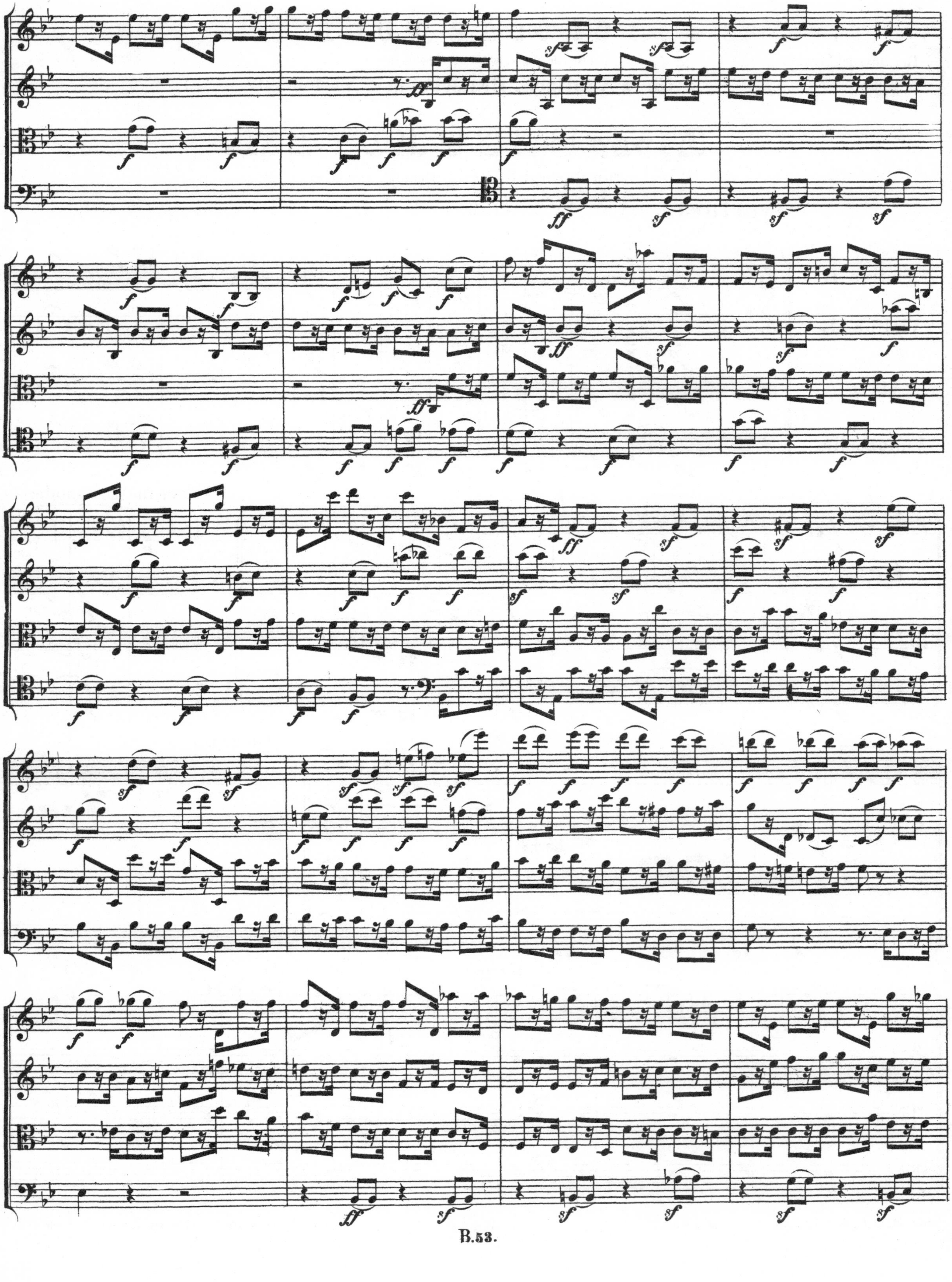

Meno mosso e moderato.

Allegro molto e con brio.

Meno mosso e moderato.

poco a poco sempre più allegro ed accelerando il tempo

dim.

poco a poco sempre più allegro ed accelerando il tempo

Allegro molto e con brio.

B.53.

Dover Orchestral Scores

Bach, Johann Sebastian, COMPLETE CONCERTI FOR SOLO KEYBOARD AND ORCHESTRA IN FULL SCORE. Bach's seven complete concerti for solo keyboard and orchestra in full score from the authoritative Bach-Gesellschaft edition. 206pp. 9 x 12. 0-486-24929-8

Bach, Johann Sebastian, THE SIX BRANDENBURG CONCERTOS AND THE FOUR ORCHESTRAL SUITES IN FULL SCORE. Complete standard Bach-Gesellschaft editions in large, clear format. Study score. 273pp. 9 x 12. 0-486-23376-6

Bach, Johann Sebastian, THE THREE VIOLIN CONCERTI IN FULL SCORE. Concerto in A Minor, BWV 1041; Concerto in E Major, BWV 1042; and Concerto for Two Violins in D Minor, BWV 1043. Bach-Gesellschaft editions. 64pp. 9⅜ x 12¼. 0-486-25124-1

Beethoven, Ludwig van, COMPLETE PIANO CONCERTOS IN FULL SCORE. Complete scores of five great Beethoven piano concertos, with all cadenzas as he wrote them, reproduced from authoritative Breitkopf & Härtel edition. New Table of Contents. 384pp. 9⅜ x 12¼. 0-486-24563-2

Beethoven, Ludwig van, SIX GREAT OVERTURES IN FULL SCORE. Six staples of the orchestral repertoire from authoritative Breitkopf & Härtel edition. *Leonore Overtures*, Nos. 1–3; Overtures to *Coriolanus, Egmont, Fidelio.* 288pp. 9 x 12. 0-486-24789-9

Beethoven, Ludwig van, SYMPHONIES NOS. 1, 2, 3, AND 4 IN FULL SCORE. Republication of H. Litolff edition. 272pp. 9 x 12. 0-486-26033-X

Beethoven, Ludwig van, SYMPHONIES NOS. 5, 6 AND 7 IN FULL SCORE, Ludwig van Beethoven. Republication of H. Litolff edition. 272pp. 9 x 12. 0-486-26034-8

Beethoven, Ludwig van, SYMPHONIES NOS. 8 AND 9 IN FULL SCORE. Republication of H. Litolff edition. 256pp. 9 x 12. 0-486-26035-6

Beethoven, Ludwig van; Mendelssohn, Felix; and Tchaikovsky, Peter Ilyitch, GREAT ROMANTIC VIOLIN CONCERTI IN FULL SCORE. The Beethoven Op. 61, Mendelssohn Op. 64 and Tchaikovsky Op. 35 concertos reprinted from Breitkopf & Härtel editions. 224pp. 9 x 12. 0-486-24989-1

Borodin, Alexander, SYMPHONY NO. 2 IN B MINOR IN FULL SCORE. Rescored after its disastrous debut, the four movements offer a unified construction of dramatic contrasts in mood, color, and tempo. A beloved example of Russian nationalist music of the Romantic period. viii+152pp. 9 x 12. 0-486-44120-2

Brahms, Johannes, COMPLETE CONCERTI IN FULL SCORE. Piano Concertos Nos. 1 and 2; Violin Concerto, Op. 77; Concerto for Violin and Cello, Op. 102. Definitive Breitkopf & Härtel edition. 352pp. 9⅜ x 12¼. 0-486-24170-X

Brahms, Johannes, COMPLETE SYMPHONIES. Full orchestral scores in one volume. No. 1 in C Minor, Op. 68; No. 2 in D Major, Op. 73; No. 3 in F Major, Op. 90; and No. 4 in E Minor, Op. 98. Reproduced from definitive Vienna Gesellschaft der Musikfreunde edition. Study score. 344pp. 9 x 12. 0-486-23053-8

Brahms, Johannes, THREE ORCHESTRAL WORKS IN FULL SCORE: Academic Festival Overture, Tragic Overture and Variations on a Theme by Joseph Haydn. Reproduced from the authoritative Breitkopf & Härtel edition three of Brahms's great orchestral favorites. Editor's commentary in German and English. 112pp. 9⅜ x 12¼. 0-486-24637-X

Chopin, Frédéric, THE PIANO CONCERTOS IN FULL SCORE. The authoritative Breitkopf & Härtel full-score edition in one volume; Piano Concertos No. 1 in E Minor and No. 2 in F Minor. 176pp. 9 x 12. 0-486-25835-1

Corelli, Arcangelo, COMPLETE CONCERTI GROSSI IN FULL SCORE. All 12 concerti in the famous late nineteenth-century edition prepared by violinist Joseph Joachim and musicologist Friedrich Chrysander. 240pp. 8⅜ x 11¼. 0-486-25606-5

Debussy, Claude, THREE GREAT ORCHESTRAL WORKS IN FULL SCORE. Three of the Impressionist's most-recorded, most-performed favorites: *Prélude à l'Après-midi d'un Faune, Nocturnes,* and *La Mer.* Reprinted from early French editions. 279pp. 9 x 12. 0-486-24441-5

Dvořák, Antonín, SERENADE NO. 1, OP. 22, AND SERENADE NO. 2, OP. 44, IN FULL SCORE. Two works typified by elegance of form, intense harmony, rhythmic variety, and uninhibited emotionalism. 96pp. 9 x 12. 0-486-41895-2

Dvořák, Antonín, SYMPHONY NO. 8 IN G MAJOR, OP. 88, SYMPHONY NO. 9 IN E MINOR, OP. 95 ("NEW WORLD") IN FULL SCORE. Two celebrated symphonies by the great Czech composer, the Eighth and the immensely popular Ninth, "From the New World," in one volume. 272pp. 9 x 12. 0-486-24749-X

Elgar, Edward, CELLO CONCERTO IN E MINOR, OP. 85, IN FULL SCORE. A tour de force for any cellist, this frequently performed work is widely regarded as an elegy for a lost world. Melodic and evocative, it exhibits a remarkable scope, ranging from tragic passion to buoyant optimism. Reproduced from an authoritative source. 112pp. 8⅜ x 11. 0-486-41896-0

Franck, César, SYMPHONY IN D MINOR IN FULL SCORE. Superb, authoritative edition of Franck's only symphony, an often-performed and recorded masterwork of late French romantic style. 160pp. 9 x 12. 0-486-25373-2

Handel, George Frideric, COMPLETE CONCERTI GROSSI IN FULL SCORE. Monumental Opus 6 Concerti Grossi, Opus 3 and "Alexander's Feast" Concerti Grossi—19 in all—reproduced from the most authoritative edition. 258pp. 9⅜ x 12¼. 0-486-24187-4

Handel, George Frideric, WATER MUSIC AND MUSIC FOR THE ROYAL FIREWORKS IN FULL SCORE. Full scores of two of the most popular Baroque orchestral works performed today—reprinted from the definitive Deutsche Handelgesellschaft edition. Total of 96pp. 8⅛ x 11. 0-486-25070-9

Haydn, Joseph, SYMPHONIES 88–92 IN FULL SCORE: The Haydn Society Edition. Full score of symphonies Nos. 88 through 92. Large, readable noteheads, ample margins for fingerings, etc., and extensive Editor's Commentary. 304pp. 9 x 12. (Available in U.S. only) 0-486-24445-8

Mahler, Gustav, DAS LIED VON DER ERDE IN FULL SCORE. Mahler's masterpiece, a fusion of song and symphony, reprinted from the original 1912 Universal Edition. English translations of song texts. 160pp. 9 x 12. 0-486-25657-X

Mahler, Gustav, SYMPHONIES NOS. 1 AND 2 IN FULL SCORE. Unabridged, authoritative Austrian editions of Symphony No. 1 in D Major ("Titan") and Symphony No. 2 in C Minor ("Resurrection"). 384pp. 8⅛ x 11. 0-486-25473-9

Mahler, Gustav, SYMPHONIES NOS. 3 AND 4 IN FULL SCORE. Two brilliantly contrasting masterworks—one scored for a massive ensemble, the other for small orchestra and soloist—reprinted from authoritative Viennese editions. 368pp. 9⅜ x 12¼. 0-486-26166-2

Mahler, Gustav, SYMPHONY NO. 8 IN FULL SCORE. Authoritative edition of massive, complex "Symphony of a Thousand." Scored for orchestra, eight solo voices, double chorus, boys' choir and organ. Reprint of Izdatel'stvo "Muzyka," Moscow, edition. Translation of texts. 272pp. 9⅜ x 12¼. 0-486-26022-4

Mendelssohn, Felix, MAJOR ORCHESTRAL WORKS IN FULL SCORE. Considered to be Mendelssohn's finest orchestral works, here in one volume are the complete *Midsummer Night's Dream; Hebrides Overture; Calm Sea and Prosperous Voyage Overture;* Symphony No. 3 in A ("Scottish"); and Symphony No. 4 in A ("Italian"). Breitkopf & Härtel edition. Study score. 406pp. 9 x 12. 0-486-23184-4

Dover Orchestral Scores

Mozart, Wolfgang Amadeus, CONCERTI FOR WIND INSTRUMENTS IN FULL SCORE. Exceptional volume contains ten pieces for orchestra and wind instruments and includes some of Mozart's finest, most popular music. 272pp. 9⅜ x 12¼. 0-486-25228-0

Mozart, Wolfgang Amadeus, LATER SYMPHONIES. Full orchestral scores to last symphonies (Nos. 35–41) reproduced from definitive Breitkopf & Härtel Complete Works edition. Study score. 285pp. 9 x 12. 0-486-23052-X

Mozart, Wolfgang Amadeus, PIANO CONCERTOS NOS. 1–6 IN FULL SCORE. Reproduced complete and unabridged from the authoritative Breitkopf & Hartel Complete Works edition, it offers a revealing look at the development of a budding master. x+198pp. 9⅜ x 12¼. 0-486-44191-1

Mozart, Wolfgang Amadeus, PIANO CONCERTOS NOS. 11–16 IN FULL SCORE. Authoritative Breitkopf & Härtel edition of six staples of the concerto repertoire, including Mozart's cadenzas for Nos. 12–16. 256pp. 9⅜ x 12¼. 0-486-25468-2

Mozart, Wolfgang Amadeus, PIANO CONCERTOS NOS. 17–22 IN FULL SCORE. Six complete piano concertos in full score, with Mozart's own cadenzas for Nos. 17–19. Breitkopf & Härtel edition. Study score. 370pp. 9⅜ x 12¼. 0-486-23599-8

Mozart, Wolfgang Amadeus, PIANO CONCERTOS NOS. 23–27 IN FULL SCORE. Mozart's last five piano concertos in full score, plus cadenzas for Nos. 23 and 27, and the Concert Rondo in D Major, K.382. Breitkopf & Härtel edition. Study score. 310pp. 9⅜ x 12¼. 0-486-23600-5

Mozart, Wolfgang Amadeus, 17 DIVERTIMENTI FOR VARIOUS INSTRUMENTS. Sparkling pieces of great vitality and brilliance from 1771 to 1779; consecutively numbered from 1 to 17. Reproduced from definitive Breitkopf & Härtel Complete Works edition. Study score. 241pp. 9⅜ x 12¼. 0-486-23862-8

Mozart, Wolfgang Amadeus, THE VIOLIN CONCERTI AND THE SINFONIA CONCERTANTE, K.364, IN FULL SCORE. All five violin concerti and famed double concerto reproduced from authoritative Breitkopf & Härtel Complete Works Edition. 208pp. 9⅜ x 12¼. 0-486-25169-1

Paganini, Nicolo and Wieniawski, Henri, PAGANINI'S VIOLIN CONCERTO NO. 1 IN D MAJOR, OP. 6, AND WIENIAWSKI'S VIOLIN CONCERTO NO. 2 IN D MINOR, OP. 22, IN FULL SCORE. This outstanding new edition brings together two of the most popular and most performed violin concertos of the Romantic repertoire in one convenient, moderately priced volume. 208pp. 8⅜ x 11. 0-486-43151-7

Ravel, Maurice, DAPHNIS AND CHLOE IN FULL SCORE. Definitive full-score edition of Ravel's rich musical setting of a Greek fable by Longus is reprinted here from the original French edition. 320pp. 9⅜ x 12¼. (Not available in France or Germany) 0-486-25826-2

Ravel, Maurice, LE TOMBEAU DE COUPERIN and VALSES NOBLES ET SENTIMENTALES IN FULL SCORE. *Le Tombeau de Couperin* consists of "Prelude," "Forlane," "Menuet," and "Rigaudon"; the uninterrupted 8 waltzes of *Valses Nobles et Sentimentales* abound with lilting rhythms and unexpected harmonic subtleties. 144pp. 9⅜ x 12¼. (Not available in France or Germany) 0-486-41898-7

Ravel, Maurice, RAPSODIE ESPAGNOLE, MOTHER GOOSE and PAVANE FOR A DEAD PRINCESS IN FULL SCORE. Full authoritative scores of 3 enormously popular works by the great French composer, each rich in orchestral settings. 160pp. 9⅜ x 12¼. 0-486-41899-5

Saint-Saens, Camille, DANSE MACABRE AND HAVANAISE FOR VIOLIN AND ORCHESTRA IN FULL SCORE. Two of Saint-Saens' most popular works appear in this affordable volume: the symphonic poem about the dance of death, *Danse Macabre,* and *Havanaise,* a piece inspired by a Cuban dance that highlights its languid mood with bursts of virtuosity. iv+92pp. 9 x 12. 0-486-44147-4

Schubert, Franz, FOUR SYMPHONIES IN FULL SCORE. Schubert's four most popular symphonies: No. 4 in C Minor ("Tragic"); No. 5 in B-flat Major; No. 8 in B Minor ("Unfinished"); and No. 9 in C Major ("Great"). Breitkopf & Härtel edition. Study score. 261pp. 9⅜ x 12¼. 0-486-23681-1

Schubert, Franz, SYMPHONY NO. 3 IN D MAJOR AND SYMPHONY NO. 6 IN C MAJOR IN FULL SCORE. The former is scored for 12 wind instruments and timpani; the latter is known as "The Little Symphony in C" to distinguish it from Symphony No. 9, "The Great Symphony in C." Authoritative editions. 128pp. 9⅜ x 12¼. 0-486-42134-1

Schumann, Robert, COMPLETE SYMPHONIES IN FULL SCORE. No. 1 in B-flat Major, Op. 38 ("Spring"); No. 2 in C Major, Op. 61; No. 3 in E-flat Major, Op. 97 ("Rhenish"); and No. 4 in D Minor, Op. 120. Breitkopf & Härtel editions. Study score. 416pp. 9⅜ x 12¼. 0-486-24013-4

Strauss, Johann, Jr., THE GREAT WALTZES IN FULL SCORE. Complete scores of eight melodic masterpieces: "The Beautiful Blue Danube," "Emperor Waltz," "Tales of the Vienna Woods," "Wiener Blut," and four more. Authoritative editions. 336pp. 8⅝ x 11¼. 0-486-26009-7

Strauss, Richard, TONE POEMS, SERIES I: DON JUAN, TOD UND VERKLARUNG, and DON QUIXOTE IN FULL SCORE. Three of the most often performed and recorded works in entire orchestral repertoire, reproduced in full score from original editions. 286pp. 9⅜ x 12¼. (Available in U.S. only) 0-486-23754-0

Strauss, Richard, TONE POEMS, SERIES II: TILL EULENSPIEGELS LUSTIGE STREICHE, "ALSO SPRACH ZARATHUSTRA," and EIN HELDENLEBEN IN FULL SCORE. Three important orchestral works, including very popular *Till Eulenspiegel's Merry Pranks,* reproduced in full score from original editions. Study score. 315pp. 9⅜ x 12¼. (Available in U.S. only) 0-486-23755-9

Stravinsky, Igor, THE FIREBIRD IN FULL SCORE (Original 1910 Version). Inexpensive edition of modern masterpiece, renowned for brilliant orchestration, glowing color. Authoritative Russian edition. 176pp. 9⅜ x 12¼. (Available in U.S. only) 0-486-25535-2

Stravinsky, Igor, PETRUSHKA IN FULL SCORE: Original Version. Full-score edition of Stravinsky's masterful score for the great Ballets Russes 1911 production of *Petrushka.* 160pp. 9⅜ x 12¼. (Available in U.S. only) 0-486-25680-4

Stravinsky, Igor, THE RITE OF SPRING IN FULL SCORE. Full-score edition of most famous musical work of the 20th century, created as a ballet score for Diaghilev's Ballets Russes. 176pp. 9⅜ x 12¼. (Available in U.S. only) 0-486-25857-2

Tchaikovsky, Peter Ilyitch, FOURTH, FIFTH AND SIXTH SYMPHONIES IN FULL SCORE. Complete orchestral scores of Symphony No. 4 in F Minor, Op. 36; Symphony No. 5 in E Minor, Op. 64; Symphony No. 6 in B Minor, "Pathetique," Op. 74. Study score. Breitkopf & Härtel editions. 480pp. 9⅜ x 12¼. 0-486-23861-X

Tchaikovsky, Peter Ilyitch, NUTCRACKER SUITE IN FULL SCORE. Among the most popular ballet pieces ever created; available in a complete, inexpensive, high-quality score to study and enjoy. 128pp. 9 x 12. 0-486-25379-1

von Weber, Carl Maria, GREAT OVERTURES IN FULL SCORE. Overtures to *Oberon, Der Freischutz, Euryanthe* and *Preciosa* reprinted from authoritative Breitkopf & Härtel editions. 112pp. 9 x 12. 0-486-25225-6

Available from your music dealer or write for ***free*** *Music Catalog to*
Dover Publications, Inc., Dept. MUBI, 31 East 2nd Street, Mineola, NY 11501
Visit us online at ***www.doverpublications.com***